John Hamlin Dewey

Sons of God and Brothers of Christ

John Hamlin Dewey

Sons of God and Brothers of Christ

ISBN/EAN: 9783743317246

Manufactured in Europe, USA, Canada, Australia, Japa

Cover: Foto ©Lupo / pixelio.de

Manufactured and distributed by brebook publishing software
(www.brebook.com)

John Hamlin Dewey

Sons of God and Brothers of Christ

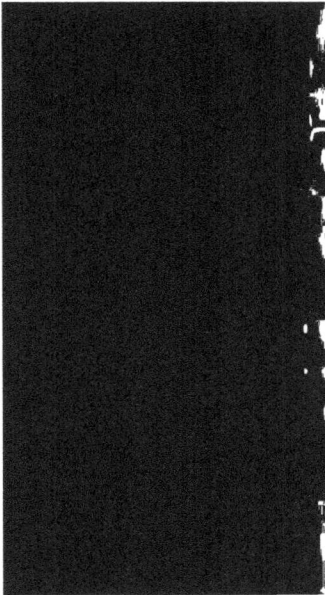

OF GOD

ND

HERS OF

RIST

PRICE, 25 CENTS

Sons of God

and

Brothers of Christ

BY

JOHN HAMLIN DEWEY, M.D.

AUTHOR OF

"THE WAY, THE TRUTH AND THE LIFE," "THE PATHWAY OF THE SPIRIT,"
"THE OPEN DOOR, OR THE SECRET OF JESUS," "DAWNING DAY,"
"THE GENESIS AND EXODUS OF THE HUMAN SPIRIT,"
"THE NEW TESTAMENT OCCULTISM," ETC.

"For as many as are led by the Spirit
of God, they are the Sons of God"

NEW YORK

THE J. H. DEWEY PUBLISHING CO.

1896

SONS OF GOD AND BROTHERS OF CHRIST.

For the Earnest Expectation of the Creature Waiteth for the Manifestation of the Sons of God. (Romans 8 : 19.)

Call no man your father upon the earth: for one is your Father, which is in heaven.

Neither be ye called masters: for one is your Master, even Christ; and all ye are brethren. (Matt. 23 : 8, 9.)

Be ye therefore perfect, even as your Father which is in heaven is perfect. (Matt. 5 : 48.)

The hour cometh, and now is, when the true worshippers shall worship the Father in spirit and in truth: for the Father seeketh such to worship him.

God is Spirit: and they that worship him must worship him in spirit and in truth. (John 4 : 23, 24.)

In the above significant utterances we have the basic teaching of the one supreme Master, the most divinely illumined Teacher our world has known. No higher authority in spiritual matters is either needed or possible to us. He spake not from the inductions of a speculative philosophy, but from the God-anointed vision of a Seer. He spake that which

He knew and testified of that which He had seen. " He spake as one having authority, and not as the scribes." It was the authority of a living experience. He appealed to no law or principle the truth of which He was not himself the practical demonstration. He lived the Gospel He proclaimed, hence, " his word was with power." He was indeed " the sent of God," and " he whom God hath sent speaketh the words of God."

Here then, we have, in the supreme example and perfect teaching of the Master, a sure foundation and safe Leader. Let us give this basic teaching of the Great Master a few moments' earnest and careful consideration. If, as Jesus taught, God, as pure Spiritual Being, immanent and transcendent, is the supreme Reality, and we are His direct offspring, then we ourselves are deific beings, and have inherent and potential within us the nature and attributes of God, our heavenly Father. Theoretically, in a sort of blind, non-vital way, this doctrine has been accepted by vast numbers of men, but how few have had any realizing sense of the stupendous possibility it involves.

If we are really the children of God, in the practical sense here implied, two doors of transcendent possibility are open to us. First, we have of necessity the inherent capacity to know God in the true nature of His Being, to know Him as our Father;

and to hold as decided conscious communion and fellowship with Him in this inborn and indestructible relationship, as we have to know and commune with one another as His children. What an exalted and exalting privilege and experience is thus open to us, and yet how few have been awakened to any vital sense of either its sublime possibility, or its unspeakable value and importance.

Second, we have by the same necessity, the inborn capacity to MANIFEST the God-nature, which is nothing less than to achieve and assert our rightful deific supremacy of being, as Sons of God and Brothers of Christ. " And God said, Let us make man in our image, after our likeness; and let them have dominion." But the mass of mankind are not yet conscious of God, much less of this deific nature and power latent and slumbering within them. How then shall they become thus conscious of God, and awakened to this sublime realization in practical experience of their own God-nature ?

That we do not spontaneously see and know God, as we see and know one another, and so manifest the God-nature as we do the sense-nature, is because that nature is yet latent, and in a sense slumbering within us. Yet the God-nature within us connects us as directly and vitally with the Being and kingdom of God within, behind, and above the world, as does the sense-nature with the world external to us.

THE FACT OF GOD MAKES POSSIBLE THE KNOWLEDGE OF GOD.

The possibility of the sense-consciousness and knowledge of external things, rests upon the fact of an outward world and of our organic relation thereto. In like manner the possibility of the God-consciousness, which is the knowledge of God and of our own God-nature as His offspring, rests upon the supreme fact of the Being and Kingdom of God, and of our organic and vital relation to them. Hence, as the sense-consciousness was awakened and established by the recognition of and communication with the outward world through the senses, so the God-consciousness must be awakened by the corresponding recognition of, and communication with the Being and kingdom of God through intuition—the spiritual sense of the inner man.

In the individualization or birth and establishment of our self-conscious personal identity as spiritual beings, we have the same inborn capacity to enter into and hold communication with the Being and kingdom of God within, through our inward and spiritual nature, that we have to enter into and hold communication with the outward world through our external and sense-nature.

BY REVELATION ONLY, IN ANSWER TO PRAYER.

It is, however, because the material world is external to us, and, in the true sense beneath us, that we are spontaneously active toward it and seek to master and possess it. And it is because the Being and kingdom of God are spiritual, and in the true sense, within, behind, and above us, that we cannot as an individual identity thus act upon them, but must be acted upon by them, and can, therefore, know them only through revelation from within. For this reason the revelation is not spontaneous, but must be specially desired and sought for in the prayer of silence. It can come to us only through the receptive and listening attitude, not through the positive and aggressive, and never by intellectual analysis or study. Hence it is of necessity a matter of specially awakened desire which prompts to voluntary seeking, and not, as with the senses, a spontaneous and involuntary activity.

As this direct and immediate revelation of God is necessary to the awakening of the God-nature in us, until we see and know Him as He is, we cannot, by any means, know and realize our own God-nature. We must certainly know the true nature of God as our Father, before we can realize and manifest that nature in ourselves, as His children. But, as we have seen, this knowledge comes only by revelation from within in response to our specific desire for it. Hence, true prayer—the prayer of silence—is the only door that opens the soul to the direct revelation of God, and brings thereby the realization of the God-nature in ourselves.

THE FACT OF A SPIRITUAL NATURE IN US MAKES ALL DIVINE REALIZATION POSSIBLE TO US.

We could not desire to know the nature of God and to be like Him, nor could He reveal Himself to us in His real nature as our Father, unless as His children that nature was inherent within us. Only the real nature of the Father in us could desire the touch of His Spirit, and consciously respond to it. Now the indisputable fact that men have this desire to know God, and to share in His nature and supremacy, is itself the demonstration that the God-nature is inherent within them, giving them the innate capacity to realize the full and complete fruition of this desire. " Beloved, now are we the Sons of God, but it doth not yet appear what we shall be: but we know that when he shall appear [is revealed to us], we shall be like him; for we shall see him as he is. And every man that hath this hope in him purifieth himself, even as he is pure."

What is needed, then, to bring this fruition, is to

have our desire and attention centred in inward concentration upon God, for the revelation, in sufficient intensity to overrule and bring into stillness the sensuous activities, and maintain the receptive, listening, and expectant attitude in which only the revelation can be given or received. This constitutes the effective prayer of silence.

This revelation being the most sublime and exalted knowledge and experience possible to man, it can be opened to him only in response to the supreme and all-absorbing desire of the heart for it. When this desire after God for His own sake becomes thus all-absorbing, there will be no difficulty about the concentration of attention upon Him. It will indeed be impossible to keep the attention from Him. " Where thy treasure is there will thy heart be also," and where thy heart is centred, there will thy attention be correspondingly fastened. " Ye shall seek me, and find me, when ye shall search for me with all your heart."

Since, then, we cannot become conscious of nor manifest the deific quality of our own being until we know the real nature of God as our Father, and since nothing but the conscious touch of His Spirit in response to our supreme desire for it can give the revelation and awaken this consciousness and power, the seeking of this revelation should become the first and supreme object of our life. When this determination fully dominates the soul, the revelation and realization will not be long delayed.

NO OBJECTIVE VISION OF GOD.

In seeking this revelation or vision of God, however, we must remember that " God is Spirit," and so invisible and ubiquitous Being, an Omni-Holy Presence in which " we live, move, and have our being." Hence this " beatific vision " or vision of God, is not an objective vision as of some being or object external to us, or even a symbolic picture to the inner or psychic vision; for God is not form to be objectively or externally seen, or symbolized by anything in the heavens above or earth beneath, or by anything the imagination can conceive.

" God is Spirit," said the Master, and, as such, is both immanent and transcendent Being, within, behind, and above all things—the inward life and over-ruling power and providence. This should emphasize in our mind the one supreme thing of incalculable importance to every human soul, which is, that the awakening to the consciousness of our God-nature by the quickening touch of the Father's Spirit, brings with it the realization of our deific supremacy of being in and over our physical organism, and over all our sense relations to the world external to ourselves.

REVEALED TO INTUITION.

But it will be asked, If God is in no sense external to us, and cannot thus be perceived, how is a vision of or revelation from Him possible ? We answer, that just as man has objective perception or sense vision, the power to perceive the form and externals of things, so he has intuition, an interior spiritual perception or apprehension of the qualities which inhere in the nature of things.

This intuition is spontaneously active in greater or less degree with all people, yet being unrecognized and uncultivated, as such, by the great majority, its activities become so mingled with the inductions from sense impressions as to become obscured and indistinct. Yet in spite of this, its action often becomes too clear and incisive to the consciousness to be ignored, and then its authority rises above all power of sense impressions to quench. It then reflects and expresses the truth in its separateness, and is thus the voice of God in the soul.

Only through the awakened intuition can we have the revelation of God and know the truth of being. The true vision of God is thus a revelation to the intuitive perception of the qualities or nature of His Being, rather than any form of existence capable of being observed and studied.

KNOWN IN REALIZATION.

Intuition being a function of the spiritual nature and not of the sense mind, this apprehension of the qualities and nature of Divine Being from the revelation of God to the intuition, is not, strictly speaking, an intellectual apprehension. It is more an inward spiritual realization. The very desire to know God involves the desire to realize His nature within us, as we can know Him only by and in this realization. Indeed the desire itself is the stirring of the God-nature within us calling for and responding to its own; and only as this desire for God and for conscious identification with Him rises above the desires of self and sense, do we open ourselves to this emancipating revelation of God to our souls, giving not only the consciousness of God as our Father, but of our own deific nature as His children.

The knowledge of God and His attributes as an abstract proposition to the intellect, is but a vain and empty speculation, having no vitalizing influence upon the life. But the knowledge of God through intuition, by direct revelation in response to the heart's supreme desire for it, is itself the vital apprehension of the very nature of God, which gives the inward realization and controlling consciousness of our own God-nature.

It will thus be seen that God in His real nature and Being cannot be found or realized through any degree of philosophical induction or metaphysical analysis, any more than love can thus be found and realized. The knowledge of God, like the knowledge of love, comes to the soul by revelation only, " for God is Love." It is indeed the love of the Father penetrating the heart of His child, and the response of the heart of the child to the Father's love. " We love him because He first loved us." It is the response of one conscious and loving being to another. This supreme knowledge must therefore be sought and found through the heart and by desire or prayer, rather than through the intellect by metaphysical analysis and philosophical induction and mastery.

It will also be seen that the nature of God can be perceived and apprehended only through an interior and subjective realization within ourselves of what Divine Being is. Nothing short of this constitutes a true revelation. And it is because we are spiritual beings and children of God, and the substance of our essential being is His nature in us, that we have the capacity for this supreme revelation in realization. Hence it is, we repeat, an inward revelation of the nature of God as Supreme Being, to our own interior being, which gives us not only the consciousness of the Being of God as our Father, but awakens the God-consciousness in us, which, as we have said, is the realization of our own deific supremacy of being.

All that blinds us, or shuts out this higher deific consciousness now, is the dominance of the sense life and its consciousness, by which we are held in bondage to its limitations. And nothing but the supremacy of the heart's desire centred upon the things of the sense life, holds us in this bondage to the life of sense and the limitations of its consciousness.

The awakening of a still deeper desire to know God and the things of the Spirit of God, and to be identified with His kingdom as the supreme good (making these the real treasure of our hearts), will open us to the immediate revelation of the Being and kingdom of God, and bring the realization of His nature in ourselves.

This realization will bring self and sense into complete and permanent subjection to the divine and impersonal ego, and the law of the Spirit in the personal life.

How can this awakening revelation of God be made, and the transforming influence of His Spirit be felt or exerted in and upon our life, while our desires and attention are centred upon self and the things that minister to self, and not upon God for this revelation and the emancipating touch and transforming power of His Spirit ? The question is its own answer. " They that are after the flesh do mind the things of the flesh; but they that are after the Spirit, the things of the Spirit."

THE LAW OF THE SPIRIT OF LIFE.

" The law of the Spirit of life in Christ Jesus," said Paul, " hath made me free from the law of sin and death. For what the law could not do, in that it was weak through the flesh, God sending his own Son [the true and loyal one] in the likeness of sinful flesh, and for sin, condemned [not the flesh, but] sin in the flesh: that the righteousness [requirement] of the law might be fulfilled in us, who walk not after the flesh, but after the Spirit."

What was this emancipating law of the Spirit of life in Christ Jesus ? and what the law of sin and death to which the Apostle referred ? Surely it was love for God and for the pure and holy life in Him, that constituted the law of the Christ-life in Jesus. " Now if any man have not the Spirit of Christ, he is none of his." The law of sin and death from which the Apostle was delivered, and from which all must be delivered before they can live the true, masterful, and perfect life of a Son of God and

2

Brother of Christ, was love of self and of the things that minister to self. This is the law of the animal nature, or " mind of the flesh," and right for the animal who has no higher nature, but fatal for man, whose higher nature allies him to God and makes possible to him the nobler, spiritual, and perfect life (morally and physically) of a Son of God. " For the mind of the flesh is death; but the mind of the Spirit is life and peace: because the mind of the flesh is enmity against God; for it is not subject to the law of God, neither indeed can it be: and they that are in the flesh cannot please God. But ye are not in the flesh, but in the Spirit, if so be that the Spirit of God dwelleth in you. . . . But if the Spirit of him that raised up Jesus from the dead dwelleth [abideth] in you, he that raised up Christ Jesus from the dead shall quicken [transform and make perfect] also your mortal bodies through his spirit that dwelleth in you. So then, brethren, we are debtors, not to the flesh, to live after the flesh [the animal nature was designed to serve, not to rule in the human economy]: for if ye live after the flesh, ye must die; but if by the Spirit ye put to death the deeds of the body [bring the flesh into subjection to the Spirit], ye shall live. For as many as are led by the Spirit of God, these are the Sons of God." (Romans, 8th Ch., New Version.)

OUR SPIRITUAL NATURE DEMANDS GOD.

So it will be seen that the revelation of God, with its emancipating and transfiguring power, can come to us only in response to the supreme desire of our hearts for it, which is the desire of the spiritual nature that calls for the things of the Spirit, as against the animal nature, or mind of the flesh, which clings to and seeks the things of the sensuous life as its supreme good.

We must set our hearts on God and the things of the Spirit of God as our supreme good, if we would have the kingdom of God opened within us and enthroned in its divine supremacy in our conscious life. The desires and demands of our spiritual nature must rise above those of the animal within us, and if we would cultivate the spiritual nature so as to deepen, strengthen, and intensify its desires and demands till they become supreme, we must turn our attention from the sensuous life to the things of the Spirit. " For they that are after the flesh do mind [cling to] the things of the flesh; but they that are after the Spirit, the things of the Spirit."

THE NATURE AND FUNCTION OF PRAYER.

The dominant desire of our heart focussed in a mental picture of the thing desired and longed for,

is the only real prayer, and the prevailing desire
that dominates our life is the prayer of our life,
and this prayer is always practically answered.
" Ask, and it shall be given you; seek, and ye shall
find; knock, and it shall be opened unto you. For
every one that asketh receiveth; and he that seeketh
findeth; and to him that knocketh it shall be
opened." This dominant desire or prayer of our life
is what we are constantly sowing, whether it be to the
flesh or to the Spirit, and we must inevitably reap
what we sow. " Be not deceived: God is not mocked.
Whatsoever a man soweth that shall he also reap.
He that soweth to his own flesh, shall of the flesh reap
corruption; and he that soweth to the Spirit shall of
the Spirit reap life everlasting." " For to be carnally
minded is death; but to be spiritually minded is life
and peace."

Since, then, we reap what we sow, and our real
prayers are practically answered, and since our dominant desire constitutes our real prayer, it becomes
us to see carefully to it that our prayer or supreme
desire is centred upon that, which received, will be
to our highest good and well-being. Are we really
praying for the kingdom of God to come and His
will to be done in our conscious lives as it is in
heaven ? Or is the love and will of self the motive
spring of all our prayers ?

The dominance of the sensuous life over the

spiritual, or of the animal nature or "mind of the flesh," over "the mind of the Spirit," need not necessarily be manifest in the grosser sensual indulgence of the fleshly appetites and passions. There is a refined sensualism that rises to the highest plane of the poetic and æsthetic culture of the personal ego, in which self-love is still the foundation spring of motive and inspiration. There is not only the "lust of the flesh," but there is also " the lust of the eyes and the pride of life, which are not of the Father but of the world."

MIND OF THE SPIRIT VERSUS MIND OF THE FLESH.

All have the mind of the Spirit, and all may, therefore, with this mind of the Spirit, recognize and admire the things of the Spirit—love, mercy, justice, truth, purity, and the spirit of the unself—as infinitely above the things of flesh and sense, and with the spiritual mind really desire these things. Yet all have also the mind of the flesh, and with this mind will necessarily desire the things which minister to self and sense.

If the desires of this sensuous mind rise above and dominate those of the spiritual mind, however much we may recognize, admire, appreciate and even desire the things of the Spirit, this dominance of self which would appropriate the gifts of the Spirit to personal ends, is what we really sow and reap, and the prayer that brings its answer in our life.

We may even sufficiently recognize and appreciate the transcendent value and advantage of union with God and the life it gives, to actually desire and pray for them, and yet the subtle spirit of self be so insinuated within and behind this prayer as the spring of its motive, that our desire for the mastery which belongs to this higher life of the Spirit, the exaltation which it would, if attained, bring to self, is really what we pray for. It is but the self-deceptive prayer of the personal ego, seeking union with God not as an end, but a means to the end of personal aggrandizement. It is of the spirit of the world in us, not of the kingdom of God.

The deep spiritual insight of the inspired and beloved Apostle, enabled him to draw a clear-cut line of distinction at this critical point of experience where so many fail through self-deception. "Love not the world, neither the things that are in the world. [The things upon which our hearts are set as our chief good, are what we really love.] If any man love the world, the love of the Father is not in him. For all that is in the world, the lust of the flesh, and the lust of the eyes, and the pride of life, is not of the Father but is of the world. And the world passeth away, and the lusts thereof: but he that doeth the will of God abideth forever."

THE DOING OF GOD'S WILL NOT AN ARBITRARY DEMAND BUT A BENEFICENT PRIVILEGE.

A true and loyal child because of his love for the father or mother, will of his own free choice and volition make their desire for him the law of his life. His confidence also in the superior wisdom of their judgment over his, leads him to cheerfully and even gladly subordinate his judgment to theirs, knowing that they have his own best good in view.

If, however, a child had reason to believe that his parents had not his best good in view (which he had a right to expect of them), but were using him to their own selfish ends and to his hurt, justice and truth would not demand the cheerful and glad subordination of his will and judgment to theirs, simply because they were his parents, even though he might be obliged to submit to their arbitrary demands because he was in their power. There is quite as imperative a demand that the parent be loyal to the best interest of the child, which, if he has a true love for the child he will be, as that the child be loyal to the parent through filial love and confidence.

When parental love is recognized by the child, a true love and confidence toward the parent will be awakened, which will spontaneously make the parental will and plan, so far as understood, the supreme law of its life and action, even to the prompt and persistent denial and sacrifice of every personal desire which is seen to be contrary thereto. Certainly the perfection of his own character and life, and so the realization of his highest well-being, could only thus be secured.

Applying this law and principle to the relation of man to God as child to Parent, in the recognition of the absolute wisdom and goodness of the Father, all arbitrariness disappears from the demand that the will of God should become the actual law of the personal and social life of man as the child of God, since the demand itself is based upon the spontaneous loyalty of the child-love in man for God as the Father, and his faith and trust in the Father's perfect goodness and providence, and not upon the dread of any arbitrary enforcement of that will against his desire.

THE DUALITY OF MAN A KEY TO THE PROBLEM.

It is the spiritual nature in man which is the real child of God, not the animal or sense-nature, which is as truly the child of nature, or of the world spirit. The spiritual man is the man of the Father's nature, and is ever spontaneously loyal to that nature and cannot be otherwise, because this is the very law and necessity of his nature, just as the animal nature is true and loyal to the spirit of the world, because this is its nature and the necessary expression of it. Both of these natures are in man; the one dominates the personal ego which is thus ruled by the spirit of the world, the other dominates the impersonal ego which is ruled by the love of the Father.

The animal nature is a necessity to the physical organism, and when held to its subordinate functions in the human economy, is of divine appointment. But when allowed to dominate the personal life, the law of the animal nature, which is self-seeking and self-indulgence, or pleasure as an end, over-rules the law of the human nature, which, as the child of God, is duty and achievement as an end, and pleasure only in these.

PERVERTED DESIRE CONSTITUTES LUST.

The perversion of the normal life of man as the child of God, corrupts that life and brings it into subjection to the world spirit through lust, which is perverted desire, causing perverted activities of mind and body. On the plane of the fleshly appetites and propensities, this perversion produces the " lust of the flesh," by the prostitution of these functions to the ends of animal indulgence. On the plane of the social life and its relations, it comes forth in covetousness or the " lust of the eyes," the desire for possession to personal ends or the greed of gain for its own sake, still rooted in the spirit of self. On the plane of the individual career and achievement it is manifest in "the pride of life," the egoism and vanity of personal distinction as something more and better than others, the desire for and love of worldly honor, position, and power, even to the sacrifice, if need be, of others' good.

In all these we see the dominance of the spirit of self, or the personal ego ruled by the worldly spirit. It is the law of the animal nature dominating the human life to the perversion of its powers, and " is not of the Father," nor of His Son (the impersonal ego) in us, " but of the world," through the clinging of the desires of the dominant personal ego to the spirit and things of the world. " If any man love the world, the love of the Father is not in him." " No man can serve two masters."

The recognition and love of God as the Father involves the corresponding recognition and love of man as brother. The realization of either is impossible without the corresponding realization of the other. When this law and spirit, which is of the Father, rules, there will be no desire for distinction, possession, or indulgence which cannot be shared by all to mutual advantage and happiness.

All the evils that afflict mankind are " the corruptions that are in the world through lust," born of the dominant selfish spirit of the personal ego. Hence when the impersonal ego supplants the personal ego, or the spirit of love and service, which is the spirit of brotherhood, supplants this spirit of self, every evil in the world will disappear forever; and the kingdom of heaven, or of harmony and love, in all their fulness of blessing, will be enthroned in human life and society on earth, in the full " manifestation of the Sons of God."

THE HUMAN BODY A TEMPLE OF DIVINITY.

The physical organism was a necessity to the individualization, through embodiment, of the human soul as a spiritual being and child of God, and is designed to be a complete organic instrument for the external manifestation and expression of the inherent deific powers of the soul. When it is used only to the ends of these higher activities, it will be such an instrument, and will perfectly respond to every demand made upon it by the soul, in the full realization of its deific nature and powers. But when yielded up to the demands of the animal, in self-indulgence, it becomes utterly unfitted as the organic instrument of these high functions.

We have said also that the animal nature was a necessity to this physical organism, and when held to its subordinate function in the human economy (as servant, not master), was of divine appointment. The law of the animal life is pleasure as an end, and this for the animal is found mostly in physical sensation, and results in the unrestrained indulgence of his animal impulses and propensities, fear being the only restraining influence over him. This is right for the animal and in no way prejudicial to his health and well-being; while in man it is destructive to both.

The organism of the animal is constructed in reference to this law as this is the only source of his enjoyment and delight. It is the reverse with man; his physical organism is constructed with direct and special reference to the higher activities of his mental and spiritual powers, the animal functions in his physical economy to be subordinated to these higher activities, their normal action being thus made subservient to this end.

The strictly animal functions in man are a necessity to the preservation of the physical organism as an instrument for the use of the higher functions and activities of the soul, and to the perpetuation of the race. When indulged or exercised only to these ends, they contribute to his highest good, as the energy which would otherwise be wasted in unnecessary animal indulgence is conserved and expended on the higher plane of the nobler human activities, to the development and perfection of both soul and body. But let the animal dominate the human, and the physical organism thus be made the instrument of animal indulgence as an end, or for its own sake, the health of the body becomes thereby impaired and often utterly wrecked; and the soul deprived of its normal conditions for the bringing forth and activity of its nobler powers. Even if the grosser indulgences or lusts of the flesh be, from any motive, restrained, yet this law of the animal nature, which is self-seeking and self-indulgence, or pleasure as an end, be still allowed to dominate the personal life on its higher planes of activity, it will, as we have seen, pervert and corrupt the entire life to the ends and spirit of self.

SUBORDINATION, NOT DESTRUCTION OF THE ANIMAL NATURE IN MAN.

It is not, then, the destruction of the animal nature and functions in man, but its subordination to the human under the law of the Spirit in the life, that is needed for the perfection of that life. The personal life must be emancipated and redeemed " from the corruptions that are in the world through lust," whether it be " the lust of the flesh, the lust of the eyes, or the pride of life, which are not of the Father, but of the world." This is the salvation proposed and promised in the Christ-gospel.

The spirit of self generated from the dominance of the animal nature in the sense life, which Paul calls "the mind of the flesh," and which, ruling in man, he calls "the law of sin and death," must be overcome and rooted out before man can live his true life in "the manifestation of the Sons of God."

"MARK OF THE BEAST."

This spirit of self is the real serpent nature referred to in the symbolic story of Eden as more subtle than all the beasts of the field which the Lord God had made, because it was generated from the lifting up and conjunction of the animal with the human, by which it took on a subtlety from contact with human intelligence unknown to the animal world. It is this subtle, self-deceiving, self-seeking, and lying spirit of the personal ego with the animal impulses lurking within and behind it, which is the only Satan and adversary of souls. This is the "old serpent," "dragon," "devil," "tempter," and "roaring lion seeking whom he may devour." It was the only devil in the temptation of Jesus in the wilderness, and the only devil referred to by Him as "the prince of this world" and "the father of lies." "Ye are of your father the devil, and the lusts of your father ye will do: he was a murderer from the beginning, and abode not in the truth, because there is no truth in him. When he speaketh a lie, he speaketh of his own: for he is a liar and the father of it." (Jno. 8 : 44.)

Under this subtle, perverting, lust-producing spirit of self, this " law of sin and death " enthroned in " the mind of the flesh," the personal ego forever stands convicted. Nothing, therefore, but the utter laying down of self will, in the supreme desire and sincere seeking to know and do only the Father's will, in the loving and loyal spirit of a true child, can open us to and unite us consciously with the Spirit and life of the Father, by which we are lifted out of self into the divine supremacy and perfection of our being in Him.

This supreme desire to forsake the life of self and sin for conscious union and fellowship with the Father in the perfect life of the unself, is the true and saving prayer which opens heaven unto us, and lets its transmuting and transfiguring Spirit as an abiding presence and power, into and upon our life, as it did to the Master at His baptism at Jordan, and to His Apostles at Pentecost. It is what the great Mystic, Wm. Law, called " The Spirit of Prayer, by which we rise out of the vanities of time into the riches of eternity," or out of the emptiness of the unsatisfying life of sense and self, into the sublime heritage of the Sons and Daughters of God, Brothers and Sisters of Christ, the true life of loyal service and divine achievement.

THE FINAL AND SUPREME TEMPTATION.

After the full revelation of the higher spiritual life of divine sonship and supremacy has broken in undimmed splendor upon the soul as its own, the final victory over self is yet, in the power of the Spirit, to be won. Even on these sublime heights of spiritual vision, revelation, and experience, the subtle spirit of self in the personal ego will rise up seeking to share this glory and subordinate it to the ends of the personal life. This is exactly what occurred to Jesus in His experience on the mount of temptation.

If this was true of the Master, no other soul seeking the higher life need expect to escape it. This is indeed where many who had reached the open vision of the Spirit have fallen. They have yielded to the great temptation of attempting to appropriate the gifts and power of the Spirit to personal ends, the ends of personal aggrandisement. The historic pathway over which aspiring souls have climbed the mountain heights of spiritual realization is strewn with the wrecks of blasted lives who fell under this great temptation.

Let every earnest seeker heed the lesson, and see to it that through self-deception he does not fail to reach the height of divine revelation and the open spiritual vision, and that having reached that momentous crisis in which the final and decisive conflict and struggle between the subtle spirit of self, and the divine unself, is to be entered, let him keep the example before him of the great Master who in the same crisis, in the power of the Spirit won the final and permanent victory through His unflinching fidelity to the unself, in supreme devotion to the Father's will.

THE SUPREME ENCOURAGEMENT.

Finally, let us all remember, that since the sublime contest and complete victory of the great Captain of our salvation, we have not only the advantage of His example and instruction, but the mighty help of His living, perpetual, spiritual ministry, promised and given to all who shall earnestly seek to follow His teaching and example. Having been " tempted in all points like as we are," and in every step gained the victory, " he is able to succor " and give all needed aid to " them that are tempted," and this promise of help and succor stands as a perpetual and unfailing promise unto all who seek it. " Who shall separate us from the love of Christ ? shall tribulation, or distress, or persecution, or famine, or nakedness, or peril, or sword ? . . . Nay, in all these things we are more than conquerors through [the help of] Him that loved us. For I am persuaded that neither death, nor life, nor angels, nor principalities, nor powers, nor things present, nor things to come, nor height, nor depth, nor any other creature, shall be able to separate us from the love of God, which is in Christ Jesus our Lord." (Romans 8 : 35, 39.)

We can descend to no depth of sin and shame, nor ascend to any height of attainment where we may not have, when desired, the helping hand and loving sympathy and friendship of our divine Brother and ascended Lord. " God hath made that same Jesus whom ye have crucified both Lord and Christ," by which He is spiritually enthroned in a perpetual and perfect saving ministry to men, leading and directing a mighty host who are one with Him in this blessed unfailing ministry of heaven. " Are they not all ministering spirits, sent forth to minister for them who shall be heirs of salvation ? "

The revealing and illuminating Spirit of the Father from within the soul, and the helping Christ ministry of heaven from without the soul, are seeking us with infinitely more solicitude than we are seeking God, and are ever ready, through our personal co-operation with them, to help at once and completely every truly seeking soul, to the full fruition of its desire God-ward. But this desire must be absolutely centred on God, trustingly accepting whatever is sent of God: for it is to bring men to the Father that the Christ ministry is given.

Our heavenly Father is more willing and ready to give his Holy Spirit to them that ask Him, than we are to give good gifts to our children. This is the unqualified assurance of the Master, who had himself proved its truth in practical experience. But He everywhere emphasized this gift of the Father, as the one " pearl of great price " for which a man must sell, or yield all that he hath to obtain. While the heart is centred on anything less, it has no room for this most precious gift.

THE SUPREME POSSESSION.

The Christ-gospel was the promised possession of the kingdom of God, or the opening of that kingdom in our conscious life now and here. His emphasis was, therefore, to make this possession the first object and aim of our life effort, and be anxious for nothing else. Be not anxious even about the necessary things of the physical life, " For your heavenly Father knoweth that ye have need of all these things. But seek ye first his kingdom and his righteousness, and all these things shall be added unto you."

In seeking the emancipated life of the Spirit in union and fellowship with God, we should not even think of the spiritual gifts that come to us as the result of that life. We must seek the life of union and fellowship with God for its own sake, in which His will and purpose for us as His children is the perfect law, and our supreme good. This is the only true life of a child of God.

If while seeking that life we emphasize in our thought the spiritual gifts with which we are to be endowed for service, we cannot help identifying them in thought with our personal activities in the outward life, and this appeals to the personal ego and tends to keep active the spirit of self. Until we come to know God and the fulness of His purpose in our life, all other considerations should, while seeking these, be ruled out of our thought. With the revelation of God and His will concerning us—which the seeking in this attitude if persisted in will bring—will come also the gifts and the knowledge of His will and of our real service in them.

The promised gifts of the Spirit are unquestionably for all who enter into the full glory of the spiritual life, and will come to each in due time; but these are only incidental to that life, not its substance or its glory. The real glory and grandeur consist in our conscious oneness with God and the knowledge of His nature as our Father, and the consequent realization of His nature and quenchless love in ourselves as His children. In

this realization we are made partakers of His goodness and sharers of His wisdom and the power which
these confer, being henceforth directly taught of
Him through inward illumination and perpetual
revelation. " It is written in the prophets, And they
shall be all taught of God." (John 6 : 45.)

ACHIEVEMENT, NOT ATTAINMENT, THE END.

When this conscious life in God is fully entered
upon, all struggle for attainment and acquisition is
at an end. In conscious oneness and fellowship with
the Father, all anxiety and effort in our own
strength ceases in the realization that all that the
Father hath is ours, as a free gift to His children,
to the full extent of our ever unfolding capacity to
receive and use, and becomes practically ours by the
using.

It is only when this point is reached that the true
life of achievement and ministry begins. As the
desire and struggle for acquisition and attainment
finally cease, these henceforth are replaced by
achievement and service. The truly emancipated
Sons and Daughters of God go forth not to be
ministered unto but to minister. From that time
they become co-workers with the Father not only in
the development of their own sublime career and
destiny, but in bringing to fruition and perfection

the potential glories and possibilities of His creation, or so much of it as the full circle of their
ever expanding sphere of relationship shall connect
them with.

THE PRAYER OF SILENCE.

The prayer of silence in which alone the full revelation of God can come, through which we are
enabled to enter into this transcendent realization of
being, is something more than outward stillness and
indefinite passivity in the silence. It means the absolute stilling of every activity and consideration
of self, with the heart centred upon God in an all-
absorbing desire for the realization of Himself and
His will, and an unflinching determination, with
His help, to do that will and that only.

This perfect and effective prayer of silence may
at first seem a most difficult thing to attain, and
many may think it useless for them to attempt it.
But let no one be disheartened at the seeming
difficulty. It is more in the seeming than reality,
and is based upon a misapprehension of the law
involved.

Let it be remembered that this very mental attitude and act is the simple and spontaneous expression of the spiritual nature and mind of the Spirit
which are in every man. Man as man and child of
God would be impossible without a spiritual nature

and its mind.   It is these which lift him above the
brute and make him man.   They are the very substance and groundwork of his essential being.   All
that hinders the normal expression of them in the
personal life of any man, is the dominance of the desires and mind of the flesh.   All that is needed, then,
to remove this hindrance and overcome the difficulty, is to strengthen, deepen, and intensify the
desires and demands of the spiritual mind (which
are for God and the things of the Spirit), until they
rise above and subdue those of the mind of the flesh,
and bring them into subjection to the law of the
Spirit, denying them indulgence from the start.
" If any man will come after me let him deny himself, and take up his cross daily, and follow me."
" If ye through the Spirit do mortify the deeds of the
body ye shall live.   For as many as are led by the
Spirit of God they are the Sons of God."   " The
mind of the flesh is death; but the mind of the Spirit
is life and peace."

NOT DIFFICULT WHEN REALLY DESIRED.

This change from the dominance of the mind of
the flesh to that of the mind of the Spirit, is readily
effected if one really desires it.   To lessen and subdue the desires of the flesh, or the desires of the
mind of the flesh in the perverted activities on the

higher planes of the sensuous life, and at the same time cultivate, strengthen, and intensify the mind of the Spirit in its nobler demands and activities, we must turn our attention from the things of the fleshly and sensuous life, to those of the spiritual life. " For they that are after the flesh do mind the things of the flesh; but they that are after the Spirit the things of the Spirit."

The continual indulgence of " the lust of the flesh, the lust of the eyes, and the pride of life," or the perverted activities of the sensuous life which constitutes " the mind of the flesh," but strengthen and confirm them as a controlling habit of life. This necessarily renders both mind and body unfit instruments for the expression of the spiritual nature and the mind of the Spirit. And to dwell in thought upon the ephemeral, exciting, and abnormal pleasures of these destructive indulgences, but strengthens and intensifies the abnormal desire for them.

The practice of self-denial and diversion of attention from the things and transitory pleasures of sense, by centring it upon God and the things of the Spirit, until the habit of indulgence is broken, will destroy the desire for and pleasure in them. These will then be replaced by the normal desires of the spiritual man, and the higher and enduring joy and gladness of spiritual freedom and supremacy in a life of divine and heavenly communion and fellowship, to which this very self-denial and changed attitude open us.

The cultivation and enjoyment of this higher life of spiritual experience and heavenly inspiration is open and possible to all, in greater or less degree, even before the desires and mind of the flesh are subdued and the lusts thereof rooted out. It should, therefore, be entered upon at once, though the denied fleshly desires and the seducing enticements of the sensuous life upon which we are turning our backs, are clamoring through the recurring power of habit with almost resistless appeal for our attention and indulgence. Divine and Omnipotent help is ours for the asking.

But there must, at the very start, be the sincere desire and unflinching determination to put forever behind us the old life and enter permanently upon the new. In the New Testament language, " Put off the old man and put on the new." This desire must be aroused and determination made as the very first step, and is the one thing of supreme importance. This step taken, the battle is half won. Until it is decidedly taken there will be continual failure.

As a specific means of strengthening our faith and intensifying desire for the nobler life of the Spirit, aside from prayer itself, there is nothing so inspiring and specially helpful as the sympathetic and

prayerful study of the life and words of the Master
and His inspired Apostles, dwelling especially upon
the wondrous promises of Him who was indeed " the
sent of God," and who therefore " spake the words
of God."   The inspired Peter refers to them as
" exceeding great and precious promises, that by
these ye might be partakers of the divine nature,
having [through the inspiration of their encourage-
ment] escaped the corruption that is in the world
through lust."   And again as a " sure word of
prophecy; whereunto ye do well that ye take heed
as unto a light that shineth in a dark place, until the
day dawn, and the day star arise in your hearts."
(2 Pet. 1 : 4 and 19.)

This individual effort is greatly helped and results hastened by the union of two or more in seasons of retirement together for little Pentecostal
groups in silent meditation and prayer and mutual
encouragement in the work, " not forsaking the
assembling of ourselves together " under the Christ
promise, that " where two of you shall agree on
earth as touching anything they shall ask, it shall
be done for them of my Father which is in heaven.
For where two or three are gathered together in
my name, there am I in the midst of them."   (Matt.
19 : 19.) *

* For instruction in spiritual gatherings or inspirational meet-
ings, see 1 Cor. 15th chapter, and " The Master's Perfect Way,"
by the author.

ABSOLUTELY A MATTER OF PERSONAL CHOICE AND VOLITION.

The putting off of the old man and putting on the new, is wholly a matter of our own desire and determination, or choice and volition. Every man has both the sense-nature, and the spiritual nature from which come "the mind of the flesh," and the "mind of the Spirit." The one connects us with the sense world, and the spirit of the world flows into and possesses us through the exercise of the mind of the flesh, and the indulgence of its lusts. The other connects us with God and the life of the heavens, and the Spirit and life of God and the heavens flow into us through the exercise of the mind of the Spirit. The choice lies with us, which shall dominate, and permanently become the ruling law of our life.

On the one hand, the dominance of the mind of the flesh over that of the Spirit perverts and renders abnormal all the functions and activities of the sense life into the lusts thereof, and shuts out the inspiration and fellowship of the divine and heavenly from the personal consciousness. On the other, the dominance of the mind of the Spirit does not destroy any of the true functions of the sense life, but redeems them from all perverted activities and the

lusts thereof, and holds them to their subordinate
position and legitimate activity in a normal and
perfect life. "This I say then," said the great
Apostle, "walk in the Spirit and ye shall not fulfil
the lusts of the flesh," "For sin shall not have dominion over you."

THE ALL-IMPORTANT HABIT.

Having, after due consideration, taken the first
decided step of choice and unflinching determination to live the life of a true Son of God and Brother
of Christ, the second and equally important and imperative step is to institute at once the practice (and
make of it a habit) of daily prayer and meditation,
taking for meditation the prophetic words and
promises of inspired teaching, as aids to the opening
of our minds and hearts to the immediate inspiration and help of the Divine in our devotions. The
inspired writings of all peoples contain these, but
the best and most directly helpful are found in our
own New Testament, especially the incomparable
parables and authoritative promises of the Master.

The very desire and determination of our hearts
and minds to seek conscious union and fellowship
with the Father, when once adopted as a permanent
choice, becomes, if sacredly held and cherished as
our supreme good, the constant and unceasing

prayer of our life which opens us to the direct influence of the Father's Spirit and the specific help
of His established and ever active heavenly ministry. But in special daily seasons of retirement, however brief these must be, in which for the time all
other activities are shut out, we intensify thereby
our spiritual life, and both emphasize our position
in it, and strengthen our hold upon it.

Nothing will so quickly and effectually destroy
the power of temptation, quench the fire of lust, and
hush the clamoring demands of the sensuous life,
which through the recurring tendency of old habit
will, until wholly overcome by the Spirit, persist in
rising up to harass and re-enslave the soul, as these
seasons of devout meditation and prayer. Instant
recourse to inward prayer at every recurring temptation, when this habit of prayer is established, will
immediately break its power and lift the soul above
it, as it brings to us the swift help of a divine co-
operative ministry, which is seeking us infinitely
more than we are seeking it, and which we open ourselves to by prayer to the Father for His saving help.

Thus turning our thought and attention from the
things of self and sense to the Father and the nobler
" things of the Spirit of God " which await and in-
vite our attention, accompanied with prayer for
divine help, will so arouse, strengthen, and intensify
our desire for them, that the enticement of sense and

the things of the selfish life will speedily lose their
hold upon us, and the mind of the Spirit become enthroned in its supremacy and rightful dominance
over the fleshly and sensuous life. It will then be
found comparatively easy to assume and hold the
true attitude in the prayer of silence, which opens us
to the complete revelation of God and the spiritual
illumination this confers.

THE FINAL AND DECISIVE VICTORY.

With this illumination thus obtained comes the
full power of the Spirit in which to meet and overcome the one supreme temptation in which the
spirit of self rises up to appropriate the glory and
power of the illuminated life to the ends of personal
ambition and glorification. The victory won here is
final and decisive, and won forever, as the real Christ
life of eternal achievement and victory is then begun. This once reached, we have in the prayer of
silence the key and open door to all divine revelation, realization, and achievement—to all the limit-
less resources of the Being and kingdom of our
Father in heaven.

In starting out for this wonderful life of a true and
loyal Son of God and Brother of Christ, in eternal
union and fellowship with the Father, all should remember that this, and nothing less than this, is the

life the Father has designed and provided for all His children through their co-operation with Him to this end.

By this privilege of co-operation with the Father, through the freedom of choice and volition He has given us, we are allowed to participate in the glory and blessedness of the achievement, and share in the outworking of our own sublime and exalted destiny as Sons of God and Brothers of Christ. To this end the Infinite Father has pledged the entire economy of His creation, and the direct inspiration, illumination, and all-sufficient help of His Holy Spirit, with which the active ministry of the Christ and all the Mighty host of the risen and glorified who are one with Him in this divine and heavenly ministry of heaven, are now identified.

ANGELIC MINISTRY A DIVINE PROVISION AND NECESSITY.

We read that when the Master, who was our earthly example in all things, was in His final struggle with His supreme temptation in the wilderness, and again in the awful test of His spiritual strength and faith in the Father, at Gethsemane, "angels ministered unto him and strengthened him." And again, when about to voluntarily surrender himself into the hands of the Roman soldiery, He said to one of His dazed and bewildered disciples: " Thinkest thou that I could not now pray to my Father, and he shall presently give me more than twelve legions of angels ? " (Matt. 26 : 53), (Luke 22 : 43), (Matt. 4 : 11.)

If the Master, who was our great Exemplar in all things, needed and received the direct help of a special heavenly ministry sent of God (and now led by Him), we need not hesitate to recognize and welcome it, if, with Him, we pray the Father that we receive only that which is sent of Him.

We should remember that the invisible soul-world, the realm of the departed, is a real world, and as vitally related to the material world in which we live, as is the soul to the body. It is a spiritual planet, interior to and transcending this outer planet, as truly as the human soul is interior to and transcends its physical embodiment.

That inner world or transcendent and indestructible spiritual planet is the permanent home of our arisen humanity; where all who have ever lived on earth are living still. The same is true of all inhabited physical planets; each has its own spiritual planet to which its individualized spirits rise on passing from the physical. In our own spiritual planet, which we are now considering, will be found all degrees of intellectual and moral advancement, from the darkness of the lower spheres up to the unspeakable glory and brightness of the celestial heaven.

While in that higher world there is no such arbitrary division as men have pictured of heaven and hell, nor any permanently fixed and unalterable conditions or states of being, there are, nevertheless, there as here, two general spheres which constitute two distinct orders of life and experience.

FINAL REDEMPTION OF THE RACE ASSURED BY ITS SOLIDARITY.

The race-life is unquestionably a solidarity, and thus an indestructible organic unity. Herein lies the capacity of one to suffer from the wrong of another, or to be healed from the virtue of another. In this law also lies the certainty of the ultimate and final redemption and perfection of the entire race, since if " one member suffer all the members suffer with it, and if one member be honored all the members rejoice in it."

Thus, if one or more of the human race should come to the full-orbed perfection of their individual lives, they would become a divine and all-mastering centre of radiating and attracting influence to lift and draw all men up to their level and fellowship, since they cannot be overcome and drawn down, but must attract and lift to themselves. In this consciousness

4

the Christ could truly say, " And I, if I be lifted up from the earth, will draw all men unto me."

TWO DISTINCT ORDERS OF LIFE.

The higher and regenerate order of the perfect human life having begun in the Christ, will extend until the whole race shall share in its fellowship. Until this divine fruition is reached, there will be the two orders existing in both worlds, on earth and in the spheres; one under the dominion of the spirit of self, living the circumscribed life of the personal ego, the other emancipated from the spirit of self, living in universal love the life of actualized brotherhood, the true life of the divine and impersonal ego.

Under this law in the upper world there is the one supreme order and sphere of the regenerate and perfected humanity, " the spirits of just men made perfect," an innumerable company of angelic beings, very gods in the majesty of their wisdom, goodness, and power. At the head and centre of this mighty brotherhood of Spirit is He who glorified and made perfect our common humanity in His own embodiment on earth, and having conquered death and hell, became the Leader of the Hosts of Heaven, and the great Captain of our Salvation.

All these, in unity with the Christ, having come into conscious oneness of life and will with the

Father, constitute the society of heaven and are permanently identified with the ministry of the Holy Spirit in unity with the Father, working for the final redemption and complete regeneration of the race, whether on earth or in the spheres beyond.

The other order constitutes a vast sphere, embracing all those who have not yet been awakened to the necessity or desire for regeneration, and those who have started on the path and are in various stages of the process of regeneration and spiritual enlightenment, not having yet reached the complete emancipation and perfection of the full-orbed personal life.

MUTUAL RELATIONSHIP AND INFLUENCE OF THE TWO WORLDS.

The vital and inseparable relation of that world with this, holds all who are in the flesh in conjunction with and more or less subject to the influence of those out of the flesh, while the dominant desires and mental states of those in the body determine, to a great degree, the character of the influences they attract and open themselves to from the soul side of life. This is true whether or not either class are conscious of this relationship and influence. It is practically the same between those in and out of the flesh, as between those in the flesh.

Multitudes of people are entirely unconscious of the silent influence they necessarily exert upon and receive from those with whom they have any degree of association.

All who attain complete regeneration in the earth life are thereby brought into inseparable union and conscious fellowship with the life of the celestial heaven or Christ-sphere. As with the Christ and His Apostles, the heavens are opened unto them and the Spirit descends and abides upon them, by which they are enabled to live the true Christ and apostolic life of divine illumination, mastery, and redemptive service.

Likewise, all who commit themselves fully to the seeking of the regenerate and perfect life of union with God and the life of the heavens, which is the Christ-life of absolute brotherhood and service, open themselves to the full power of the Christ-ministry, by which their spiritual emancipation and illumination are made speedy and certain.

When this is effected, they are held by the supremacy of the perfect life above the disturbing power of any antagonizing agency or influence, physical or psychic, while they are enabled to enter into communication with and exert an influence for good upon any order of life in both the physical and soul worlds. "In my name shall they cast out devils; they shall speak with new tongues; they shall take up serpents; and if they drink any deadly thing, it shall not hurt them; they shall lay hands on the sick, and they shall recover."

MARVELLOUS EXTENSION OF SOUL POWERS.

This opening of the higher spiritual consciousness while in the flesh, liberates the soul powers of perception and conscious activity on the psychic plane, and makes man at once a conscious inhabitant of both worlds. It especially enables him to come into direct communication with the inner side or soul of things, read the secrets of nature, and touch, and in a degree control and wield, her hidden occult forces at first hand.

It has been demonstrated that while in this world and using the physical body and its senses for external communication and fellowship, we can so develop and use the higher soul powers as to hold as perfect soul communion with one another independent of the physical senses, as we do and must after leaving the body.

Did you ever think how the departed hold communion with one another in the life after death? Unless they do hold such communion, and this at least as perfectly as here, through the senses, what would that life be worth? And if they do, by what means is it done? Surely they have no soul powers or functions added by death, for if they had it would change their nature and they would become another order of beings. Death or separation from the physical body can, at the most, only set free the inherent powers of the soul hitherto held to the limitation of sense perception and expression.

The physical body, it should be remembered, is but an organic instrument and fleshly covering of a corresponding, inner, ethereal, and indestructible organism, in which the soul as an individualized spiritual being, and self-conscious identity, is permanently embodied for a career of endless development and progress. To this inner and permanent organism the outer body holds relation similar to that which the husk holds to the " full corn in the ear," and, like the husk, is dropped when no longer needed.

PERCEPTION AND EXPRESSION STRICTLY SOUL POWERS.

The physical organs of sense perception and expression are but the external clothing of corresponding permanent soul organs. Hence these powers of perception and expression, having their real seat in the inner soul body, act at once on the soul plane, when the separation takes place between the outer physical and inner spiritual body. For as St. Paul says, " There is a natural body and there is a spiritual body."

In the inner soul world we see, hear, touch, converse, love, and have companionship with one another by means of this inner, permanent and indestructible, ethereal body and its organic senses of perception and expression, even more completely and satisfactorily than now through the physical senses; because there is no material veil to hide the light and true state of the soul. Death, so-called, does not create the soul organs of perception and expression any more than it creates the world into which the soul enters, or rather to which it is awakened, by its separation from the body. When thus deprived of the physical senses, and it can no longer give attention to the things of sense, it must perforce turn to the things and conditions of the soul world. This it can just as certainly do now, while in the body, by a corresponding diversion of attention from the sense to the soul plane, as has been demonstrated in the experience of thousands of seers.

Were not the conscious powers of perception and expression strictly soul powers, behind and transcending the physical organs, and so existing independent of them, the physical organs themselves would be of no avail, as shown in sudden death by a violent separation of soul and body. The physical organs of sense, in such cases, are for a little season perfect, but deprived of the inner soul action, do not and cannot respond to any impression from the sense world. These, therefore, being interior and inherent soul powers, remain perfect for action and service in and through the permanent soul body after its separation from the physical.

LIVING SOULS WITH BODIES, NOT BODIES WITH SOULS.

The fact that we are not physical bodies holding some indefinite thing called a soul, but are ourselves living souls, indestructible spiritual beings, with a transient physical body for service in a brief earthly experience, makes necessary also the fact that we are as really and vitally in the soul world while wearing the physical body, as after we have discarded it.

If, then, we fully recognized and realized as we should, that though clothed upon with a physical organism, we are now spiritual beings, we should find that by the very same soul powers of perception and expression with which we hold communication on the external plane with each other and the outward world, through the senses, we could, and would, independent of these senses, have just as direct and specific communication with each other on the soul plane, and also with the inner side or soul of all things.

By an extension of the same powers we should

also hold direct communication with our departed loved ones who are still as vitally connected with us by soul relationship, as before their separation from the body. And this is exactly what it is designed, and, in the constitution of our being, provided that we should do. We must do this when we leave the body, why not then learn and do it while in the body? To accomplish this we must simply learn to withdraw the attention and activity of the mind from the organs of sense and the things of the sense world, and concentrate them upon the soul plane and the things of the soul world.

When we can wholly shut out the sense world from our thought and attention and disentangle our consciousness from sense impressions we shall find ourselves in as free and open communication with the beings, things, and activities of the inner world, and with each other on the soul plane above and independent of the senses, as we now are with the outward world and each other on the external plane through the senses.

When we rise to live as spiritual instead of sensuous beings, as we some time will, this will be the common and universal experience. There will then practically be no separation of loved ones, either by physical absence on earth, or by the departure of our friends from the body, by what men call death. Space and physical conditions are nothing to the spirit, and to those living on the plane of the spiritual consciousness the communion and fellowship of loved ones will remain unbroken forever.

Does this seem incredible? To the sense man, yes, but to one whose mental vision has been opened to perceive the inherent deific attributes and possibilities of the human soul as a spiritual being, the direct offspring of God, this is seen to be the real and only thing to rightfully expect and work for. Life in this world will not be complete until this is realized. The gospel and religion of Jesus are designed to bring men to this, and when truly understood and applied will effect this result.

A HELPFUL ILLUSTRATION.

Take from a common experience, a simple illustration of this divine possibility. In a clear and cloudless day we look into the sky, and see nothing but an apparently empty vault of blue, but wait until the sun has disappeared below the western horizon and the curtain of night shrouds the earth in darkness. The things which but a few hours before we saw all around us are now hidden from view or but dimly perceived, while that blue vault above, so seemingly empty then, is now, to the same eyes, literally crowded with shining worlds, some of them of such magnitude and at such a distance as to baffle our powers of computation and measurement.

What has made this transformation? Is it the destruction of the things seen by day, and the sudden creation of the innumerable worlds revealed by night ? No, all were there in the daytime as at night. The night or darkness did not create the stars, nor the eyes with which we see them. The darkness simply shuts out the objects revealed by the daylight from our perception, and disentangles our minds from their impressions. Then the almost unlimited sweep of the night vision breaks upon the same perceptive power that in the daylight is held to the limited vision of a few objects within a narrow circle of the earth's surface.

The daylight and its vision typify the sense life and its limitations; while the night and its vision typify the inner life and the vast sweep and penetration of the same perceptive powers on the soul plane, when the thought, desire, and attention are withdrawn from the sense plane and turned in full concentration upon the stupendous realities and splendors of the inner world.

THE GRAND SECRET A SIMPLE LAW.

The secret lies in the ability (which may be acquired by all), to disentangle the mind from the dominance of sense impressions, by withdrawing and diverting the attention and mental action wholly from the sense organs and the external of things, and centring them upon the higher and interior soul plane, and the objects of the soul world, or the soul side of things. This ability, however, as previously shown, is perfectly acquired only by the awakening of the spiritual consciousness of being, referred to by Jesus as the new or second-birth.

This new and spiritual birth, or birth of the new and higher spiritual consciousness, is effected, as previously shown, only by the awakening touch and quickening power of the Father's Spirit upon ours, in response to the supreme desire of our own hearts for it. The voluntary and conscious re-union of the soul with God as child with Parent, through prayer and divine communion, is what opens the personal life to the transforming and illuminating power of the Father's Spirit, and sets it free from the bondage of self and the limitations of sense. To lead men to this is the end and aim of the Gospel of Jesus, which was announced from heaven as " Good tidings of great joy which shall be to all people."

AN ETERNAL SPRINGTIDE.

In the liberation of loyal souls by the birth-angel (misnamed death), they find themselves at once in the freedom, freshness, and buoyancy of perfect youth, in a world of beauty and delight, itself forever young in the morning glow of an eternal springtide, where they are welcomed with glad hearts by the many happy waiting ones gone before. Yes, there is joy in that heavenly life at their entrance there, as there will be for all the weary earthworn pilgrims in their glad transition from earth to heaven, save to those who pass on from a life of sin and shame. Even for these there is still a blessed ministry of hope and redemption in that " morning land " of endless life and progress, under the Good Shepherd and Bishop of Souls, who is " the same yesterday, to-day, and forever."

But, beloved! suppose our spiritual eyes and ears were open to all this now while in the body, is it not clear that the sting or dread and gloom of death would be gone, and that death would be no longer death but birth into a higher, grander, and vastly more expanded life? Not only so, but we should now consciously share in the freedom and blessedness of that life, though in the body. The supremacy of the spiritually awakened soul-life would dominate the body and hold it ever fresh, young, and buoyant with the perpetual springtide of the inner world, with which it is consciously one; while the kingdom of the inner world itself would thus dominate and glorify the outer, and the Lord's prayer be answered in the realization of the millennial glory of the kingdom of heaven on earth. " Thy kingdom come and thy will be done on earth as it is in heaven."

SCHOOL OF THE HIGHER LIFE.

SPECIAL STUDIES AND TRAINING IN THE CHRIST METHOD OF REACHING INTERIOR ILLUMINATION AND THE SPIRITUAL MASTERY OF BEING.

Conducted personally and through correspondence by
Dr. J. H. Dewey.

The Christ method of interior development and divine realization is based upon a specific attitude of mind and will toward God in an act of inward concentration of supreme desire and faith—the true prayer of silence.

This inward attitude and act, and this only, opens the soul to the kingdom of God within, unseals the deific fount of inspiration and power, and lifts the personal life into conscious oneness with the Divine. This consciousness breaks forever the circle of sensuous limitations and the dominance of self, opens the inner vision, and gives unfettered freedom to the soul's powers on every plane of their activity.

To induct the student into the secret and mastery of the true attitude of mind and will in this inward concentration, which thus admits the soul into the order of The Illuminati—Sons of God and Brothers of Christ—is the specific object of Dr. Dewey's personal teaching and correspondence lessons.

For further particulars address, with stamp, the Secretary,

E. L. C. DEWEY.
111 West 68th Street, New York.

THE OPEN DOOR;

OR, THE SECRET OF JESUS.

One of the most popular of Dr. Dewey's books, has been revised and enlarged by the addition of

Part III, " The Prayer of Silence."

This is, perhaps, the most searching and practical of anything Dr. Dewey has written. It treats of The Birth of a New Power,—How Acquired,—The Stupendous Possibility,—Cause of Failure,—The Primary Object,—Seership and Mastery,—Important Questions Answered,—The True Christ Gospel,—Prayer Necessary to Regeneration,—Regeneration a Divine Work,—Mistaken Methods, — The Right Motive Imperative,— Faith-basis versus Will-basis,—How to Avoid Self-hypnotization,—God Our Only Dependence.

Price, post-paid, Paper, 50 cts. ; Cloth, $1.00.

THE J. H. DEWEY PUBLISHING CO.,

111 West 68th Street, New York.

THE NEW TESTAMENT OCCULTISM

BY J. H. DEWEY, M. D.

" Behold, I give you power to tread on serpents and scorpions, and over all the power of the enemy; and nothing shall by any means hurt you."—Luke, 10 : 19.

The above promise, which through the centuries has seemed to be a dead letter in the Christian Church, has of late excited much attention in the minds of earnest truth seekers.

The ceaseless questionings as to the acceptance of one promise and the rejection of another, together with the indiscriminate confounding of the psychic powers and phenomena with the higher spiritual (which alone give mastery) has made some clear exposition of these differing powers and the laws of their development imperative. To meet this demand "The New Testament Occultism" was written and has effectually done the work.

The contrasting features of the Eastern Occultism with those of the New Testament are also specifically defined. A most needful work.

Price, postpaid, $1.50.

THE J. H. DEWEY PUBLISHING CO.,

111 West 68th Street, New York.

COMPLETE LIST OF
OCCULT AND MYSTIC WORKS,

BY JOHN HAMLIN DEWEY, M.D.

Christian Theosophy Series.

No. 1. THE WAY, THE TRUTH AND THE LIFE.
Cloth, gilt, - - - - - - - - - $2.00

No. 2. THE PATHWAY OF THE SPIRIT.
Paper, - - - - - - - - - - - .75
Cloth, gilt, - - - - - - - - 1.25

Mystic Science Series.

No. 1. THE OPEN DOOR; OR, THE SECRET OF JESUS.
Paper, - - - - - - - - - - - .50
.Cloth, - - - - - - - - - - 1.00

No. 2. THE DAWNING DAY.
Paper, - - - - - - - - - - - .30

No. 3. THE GENESIS AND EXODUS OF THE HUMAN SPIRIT.
Paper, - - - - - - - - - - - .30
Cloth, - - - - - - - - - - - .50

Occult Science Series.

No. 1. THE NEW TESTAMENT OCCULTISM.
Cloth, - - - - - - - - - - . 1.50

THE SCIENTIFIC BASIS OF MENTAL HEALING, - - - .10
THE NEW EDUCATION, - - - - - - - - - .10
THE MASTER'S PERFECT WAY, - - - - - - - .15
SONS OF GOD AND BROTHERS OF CHRIST, - - - - .25

Any of the above works sent, post free, on receipt of price.

Booklet No. 1, containing synopsis of the system of teaching and the scientific basis of same, sent on receipt of 2-cent stamp.

THE J. H. DEWEY PUBLISHING CO.
111 West 68th St., New York.

www.ingramcontent.com/pod-product-compliance
Lightning Source LLC
Chambersburg PA
CBHW021518090426
42739CB00007B/678